Aran Baby Afghans

by Mary Jane Protus

Leisure Arts, Inc. • Maumelle Arkansas

Table of Contents

Honeycomb & Cables

Finished Size: Approximately 38" x 50"

MATERIALS

Baby Sport Weight Yarn, approximately:
36 ounces, (1,020 grams, 4,525 yards)
Crochet hook, size E (3.50 mm) **or** size needed for gauge

GAUGE: 15 Dc and 7 rows = 3"

PATTERN STITCHES

Note: See Stitch Directory, pages 14-16.

CABLE PANEL (14 sts)
Note: Panel should be 2¼" wide.

Row 1 (Right side)**:** Work BPdc around next 2 sts, work FPdc around next st, work BPdc around next 2 sts, work F4 Cable, work BPdc around next 2 sts, work FPdc around next st, work BPdc around next 2 sts.

Row 2: Work FPdc around next 2 sts, work BPdc around next st, work FPdc around next 2 sts, work BPdc around next 4 sts, work FPdc around next 2 sts, work BPdc around next st, work FPdc around next 2 sts.

Repeat Rows 1 and 2 for pattern.

HONEYCOMB PANEL (24 sts)
Note: Panel should be 4" wide.

Row 1 (Right side)**:** (Work B4 Twist, work F4 Twist) 3 times.

Row 2: Work BPdc around next 2 sts, dc in next 4 dc, (work BPdc around next 4 sts, dc in next 4 dc) twice, work BPdc around next 2 sts.

Row 3: (Work F4 Twist, work B4 Twist) 3 times.

Row 4: Dc in next 2 dc, work BPdc around next 4 sts, (dc in next 4 dc, work BPdc around next 4 sts) twice, dc in next 2 dc.

Repeat Rows 1-4 for pattern.

POPCORN PANEL (23 sts)
Note: Panel should be 5" wide.

Row 1 (Right side)**:** Dc in next st, work Popcorn in next st, (dc in next 3 sts, work Popcorn in next dc) 5 times, dc in next dc.

Row 2: Hdc in next 23 sts.

Row 3: Dc in next 3 sts, (work Popcorn in next st, dc in next 3 sts) 5 times.

Row 4: Hdc in next 23 sts.

Repeat Rows 1-4 for pattern.

AFGHAN

Ch 205 **loosely**.

Row 1 (Right side)**:** Sc in second ch from hook and in each ch across: 204 sc.

Row 2: Ch 3, turn; dc in next sc and in each sc across.

Row 3: Ch 3, turn; work Row 1 of Cable Panel, work Row 1 of Honeycomb Panel, work Row 1 of Cable Panel, ★ work Row 1 of Popcorn Panel, work Row 1 of Cable Panel, work Row 1 of Honeycomb Panel, work Row 1 of Cable Panel; repeat from ★ once **more**, work FPdc around turning ch.

Row 4: Ch 3, turn; work **next** row of Cable Panel, work **next** row of Honeycomb Panel, work **next** row of Cable Panel, ★ work **next** row of Popcorn Panel, work **next** row of Cable Panel, work **next** row of Honeycomb Panel, work **next** row of Cable Panel; repeat from ★ once **more**, work FPdc around turning ch.

Repeat Row 4 until Afghan measures approximately 48" from beginning chain, ending by working Row 3 of Honeycomb Panel.

Last Row: Ch 3, turn; dc in next st and in each st across; do **not** finish off.

Continued on page 7.

Pretty Diamonds

Finished Size: Approximately 36" x 53"

MATERIALS

Baby Sport Weight Yarn, approximately:
30 ounces, (850 grams, 3,770 yards)
Crochet hook, size E (3.50 mm) **or** size needed for gauge

GAUGE: 15 Dc and 7 rows = 3"

PATTERN STITCHES

Note: See Stitch Directory, pages 14-16.

CABLE PANEL (21 sts)
Note: Panel should be 3½" wide.

Row 1 (Right side)**:** Work BPdc around next 2 sts, work F6 Cable, work BPdc around next 2 sts, work Popcorn in next st, work BPdc around next 2 sts, work B6 Cable, work BPdc around next 2 sts.

Row 2: Work FPdc around next 2 sts, work BPdc around next 6 sts, work FPdc around next 2 sts, ch 1, skip next Popcorn, work FPdc around next 2 sts, work BPdc around next 6 sts, work FPdc around next 2 sts.

Row 3: Work BPdc around next 2 sts, work FPdc around next 6 sts, work BPdc around next 2 sts, work Popcorn in next ch-1 sp, work BPdc around next 2 sts, work FPdc around next 6 sts, work BPdc around next 2 sts.

Row 4: Repeat Row 2.

Repeat Rows 1-4 for pattern.

DIAMOND PANEL (20 sts)
Note: Panel should be 4" wide.

Row 1 (Right side)**:** Dc in next 8 dc, work F4 Cable, dc in next 8 dc.

Row 2: Dc in next 8 dc, work BPdc around next 4 sts, dc in next 8 dc.

Row 3: Dc in next 6 dc, work B4 Twist, work F4 Twist, dc in next 6 dc.

Row 4: Dc in next 6 dc, work BPdc around next 2 sts, dc in next 4 dc, work BPdc around next 2 sts, dc in next 6 dc.

Row 5: Dc in next 4 dc, work B4 Twist, dc in next 4 dc, work F4 Twist, dc in next 4 dc.

Row 6: Dc in next 4 dc, work BPdc around next 2 sts, dc in next 8 dc, work BPdc around next 2 sts, dc in next 4 dc.

Row 7: Dc in next 2 dc, work B4 Twist, dc in next·8 dc, work F4 Twist, dc in next 2 dc.

Row 8: Dc in next 2 dc, work BPdc around next 2 sts, dc in next 12 dc, work BPdc around next 2 sts, dc in next 2 dc.

Row 9: Dc in next 2 dc, work FPdc around next 2 sts, dc in next 12 dc, work FPdc around next 2 sts, dc in next 2 dc.

Row 10: Dc in next 2 dc, work BPdc around next 2 sts, dc in next 12 dc, work BPdc around next 2 sts, dc in next 2 dc.

Row 11: Dc in next 2 dc, work F4 Twist, dc in next 8 dc, work B4 Twist, dc in next 2 dc.

Row 12: Dc in next 4 dc, work BPdc around next 2 sts, dc in next 8 dc, work BPdc around next 2 sts, dc in next 4 dc.

Row 13: Dc in next 4 dc, work F4 Twist, dc in next 4 dc, work B4 Twist, dc in next 4 dc.

Row 14: Dc in next 6 dc, work BPdc around next 2 sts, dc in next 4 dc, work BPdc around next 2 sts, dc in next 6 dc.

Row 15: Dc in next 6 dc, work F4 Twist, work B4 Twist, dc in next 6 dc.

Row 16: Dc in next 8 dc, work BPdc around next 4 sts, dc in next 8 dc.

Repeat Rows 1-16 for pattern.

AFGHAN

Ch 188 **loosely**.

Row 1 (Right side)**:** Sc in second ch from hook and in each ch across: 187 sc.

Row 2: Ch 3, turn; dc in next sc and in each sc across.

Row 3: Ch 3, turn; work Row 1 of Cable Panel, ★ work Row 1 of Diamond Panel, work Row 1 of Cable Panel; repeat from ★ 3 times **more**, work FPdc around turning ch.

Row 4: Ch 3, turn; work next row of Cable Panel, ★ work next row of Diamond Panel, work next row of Cable Panel; repeat from ★ 3 times **more**, work FPdc around turning ch.

Repeat Row 4 until Afghan measures approximately 51" from beginning chain, ending by working Row 1 of Diamond Panel.

Last Row: Ch 3, turn; dc in next st and in each st across; do **not** finish off.

EDGING

Row 1: Ch 1, turn; 3 sc in first dc, skip next dc, sc in each dc across to last st, 3 sc in last st; working in end of rows, work 286 sc evenly spaced across to beginning ch; working in free loops of beginning ch, 3 sc in first ch, skip next ch, sc in each ch across to last ch, 3 sc in last ch; working in end of rows, work 286 sc evenly spaced across; join with slip st to first sc: 952 sc.

Row 2: Do **not** turn; slip st in next sc, ch 1, sc in same st, ch 5, skip next sc, sc in next sc, (ch 5, skip next 2 sc, sc in next sc) 61 times, (ch 5, skip next sc, sc in next sc) twice, (ch 5, skip next 2 sc, sc in next sc) 95 times, (ch 5, skip next sc, sc in next sc) twice, (ch 5, skip next 2 sc, sc in next sc) 61 times, (ch 5, skip next sc, sc in next sc) twice, (ch 5, skip next 2 sc, sc in next sc) 95 times, ch 5, skip last sc; join with slip st to first sc: 320 loops.

Row 3: Ch 1, sc in same st, ★ 7 dc in next loop, (sc in next loop, 7 dc in next loop) across to next corner sc, sc in corner sc; repeat from ★ 2 times **more**, 7 dc in next loop, (sc in next loop, 7 dc in next loop) across; join with slip st to first sc, finish off.

THE TALE OF MRS TIGGYWINKLE
POOH'S BEDTIME BOOK

Open Cables

Finished Size: Approximately 36" x 53"

MATERIALS

Baby Sport Weight Yarn, approximately:
35 ounces, (990 grams, 4,400 yards)
Crochet hook, size E (3.50 mm) **or** size needed for gauge

GAUGE: 15 Dc and 7 rows = 3"

PATTERN STITCHES

Note: See Stitch Directory, pages 14-16.

CABLE PANEL (21 sts)
Note: Panel should be 3½" wide.

Row 1: (Right side): Work BPdc around next 2 sts, work F2 Cable, work BPdc around next 2 sts.

Row 2: Work FPdc around next 2 sts, work BPdc around next 2 sts, work FPdc around next 2 sts.

HONEYCOMB PANEL (12 sts)
Note: Panel should be 2½" wide.

Row 1 (Right side)**:** Work F6 Cable, work B6 Cable.

Row 2: Work BPdc around next 12 sts.

Row 3: Work B6 Cable, work F6 Cable.

Row 4: Work BPdc around next 12 sts.

Row 5: Work FPdc around next 12 sts.

Row 6: Work BPdc around next 12 sts.

Repeat Rows 1-6 for pattern.

POPCORN PANEL (11 sts)
Note: Panel should be 2½" wide.

Row 1 (Right side): Dc in next st, work Popcorn in next st, (dc in next 3 sts, work Popcorn in next st) twice, dc in next st.

Row 2: Hdc in next 11 sts.

Row 3: Dc in next 3 hdc, (work Popcorn in next hdc, dc in next 3 hdc) twice.

Row 4: Hdc in next 11 sts.

Repeat Rows 1-4 for pattern.

TWIST PANEL (8 sts)
Note: Panel should be 2" wide.

Row 1 (Right side): Dc in next 2 sts, work F4 Cable, dc in next 2 sts.

Row 2: Dc in next 2 de, work BPdc around next 4 sts, dc in next 2 dc.

Row 3: Work B4 Twist, work F4 Twist.

Row 4: Work BPdc around next 2 sts, dc in next 4 dc, work BPdc around next 2 sts.

Row 5: Work FPdc around next 2 sts, dc in next 4 dc, work FPdc around next 2 sts.

Row 6: Work BPdc around next 2 sts, dc in next 4 dc, work BPdc around next 2 sts.

Row 7: Work F4 Twist, work B4 Twist.

Row 8: Dc in next 2 dc, work BPdc around next 4 sts, dc in next 2 dc.

Rows 9 and 10: Repeat Rows 1 and 2.

Repeat Rows 1-10 for pattern.

AFGHAN

Ch 194 **loosely**.

Row 1 (Right side)**:** Sc in second ch from hook and in each ch across: 193 sc.

Row 2: Ch 3, turn; dc in next sc and in each sc across.

Row 3: Ch 3, turn; † work Row 1 of Cable Panel, work Row 1 of Honeycomb Panel, work Row 1 of Cable Panel, work Row 1 of Popcorn Panel, work Row 1 of Cable Panel, work Row 1 of Twist Panel, work Row 1 of Cable Panel, work Row 1 of Popcorn Panel, work Row 1 of Cable Panel, work Row 1 of Honeycomb Panel, work Row 1 of Cable Panel †, work Row 1 of Popcorn Panel, repeat from † to † once, work FPdc around turning ch.

Row 4: Ch 3, turn; † work **next** row of Cable Panel, work **next** row of Honeycomb Panel, work **next** row of Cable Panel, work **next** row of Popcorn Panel, work **next** row of Cable Panel, work **next** row of Twist Panel, work **next** row of Cable Panel, work **next** row of Popcorn Panel, work **next** row of Cable Panel, work **next** row of Honeycomb Panel, work **next** row of Cable Panel †, work next row of Popcorn Panel, repeat from † to † once, work FPdc around turning ch.

Repeat Row 4 until Afghan measures approximately 50" from beginning chain, ending by working Row 9 of Twist Panel.

Last Row: Ch 3, turn; dc in next st and in each st across; do **not** finish off.

EDGING

Note: Decreases are made as follows: Pull up a loop in next 2 sts, YO and draw through all 3 loops on hook.

Rnd 1: Ch 1, turn; 3 sc in first dc, sc in next dc, decrease, (sc in next 2 dc, decrease) across to last st, 3 sc in last st; working in end of rows, work 223 sc evenly spaced across; working in free loops of beginning ch, 3 sc in first ch, sc in next ch, decrease, (sc in next 2 chs, decrease) across to last ch, 3 sc in last ch; working in end of rows, work 223 sc evenly spaced across; join with slip st to first sc: 744 sc.

Note #1: Work tr as follows: YO twice, insert hook in stitch indicated and pull up a loop, (YO and draw through 2 loops on hook) 3 times.

Note #2: Work Shell as follows: Tr in sc indicated, (ch 2, tr in same sc) 4 times.

Rnd 2: Do **not** turn; slip st in next sc, ch 1, 3 sc in same st, skip next 2 sc, work Shell in next sc, (skip next 3 sc, sc in next 3 sc, skip next 3 sc, work Shell in next sc) across to within 2 sc of corner sc, ★ skip next 2 sc, 3 sc in corner sc, skip next 2 sc, work Shell in next sc, (skip next 3 sc, sc in next 3 sc, skip next 3 sc, work Shell in next sc) across to within 2 sc of corner sc; repeat from ★ 2 times **more**, skip last 2 sc; join with slip st to first sc.

Rnd 3: Slip st in next sc, ch 1, sc in same st, skip next sc, (sc, ch 3, sc) in each of next 4 ch-2 sps, ★ skip next sc, sc in next sc, (sc, ch 3, sc) in each of next 4 ch-2 sps; repeat from ★ around; join with slip st to first sc, finish off.

HONEYCOMB & CABLES

Continued from page 3.

EDGING

Note: Decreases are made as follows: Pull up a loop in next 2 sts, YO and draw through all 3 loops on hook.

Rnd 1: Ch 1, turn; 3 sc in first dc, decrease, (sc in next 2 sc, decrease) across to last st, 3 sc in last st; working in end of rows, work 219 sc evenly spaced across; working in free loops of beginning ch, 3 sc in first ch, decrease, (sc in next 2 chs, decrease) across to last ch, 3 sc in last ch; working in end of rows, work 219 sc evenly spaced across; join with slip st to first sc: 752 sc.

Rnd 2: Do **not** turn; slip st in next sc, ch 4, (dc, ch 1) twice in same st, ★ skip next sc, (dc in next sc, ch 1, skip next sc) across to next corner sc, (dc, ch 1) 3 times in corner sc; repeat from ★ 2 times **more**, skip next sc, (dc in next sc, ch 1, skip next sc) across; join with slip st to third ch of beginning ch-4.

Rnd 3: Ch 1, (sc, ch 3, sc) in first ch-1 sp and in each ch-1 sp around; join with slip st to first sc, finish off.

Popcorn Hearts

Finished Size: Approximately 36" x 51"

MATERIALS

Baby Sport Weight Yarn, approximately:
35 ounces, (990 grams, 4,400 yards)
Crochet hook, size E (3.50 mm) **or** size needed for gauge

GAUGE: 15 Dc and 7 rows = 3"

PATTERN STITCHES

Note: See Stitch Directory, pages 14-16.

RIDGE PANEL (5 sts)
Note: Panel should be ¾" wide.

Row 1 (Right side)**:** Work BPdc around next 2 sts, work FPdc around next st, work BPdc around next 2 sts.

Row 2: Work FPdc around next 2 sts, work BPdc around next st, work FPdc around next 2 sts.

Repeat Rows 1 and 2 for pattern.

POPCORN PANEL (3 sts)
Note: Panel should be ½" wide.

Row 1 (Right side}: Work BPdc around next dc, work Popcorn in next dc, work BPdc around next dc.

Row 2: Work FPdc around next st, ch 1, skip next Popcorn, work FPdc around next st.

Row 3: Work BPdc around next st, work Popcorn in next ch-1 sp, work BPdc around next st.

Repeat Rows 2 and 3 for pattern.

CABLE PANEL (12 sts)
Note: Panel should be 2" wide.

Row 1 (Right side}**:** Work B6 Cable, work F6 Cable.

Row 2: Work BPdc around next 12 sts.

Row 3: Work FPdc around next 12 sts.

Row 4: Work BPdc around next 12 sts.

Repeat Rows 1-4 for pattern.

HEART PANEL (17 sts)
Note: Panel should be 3½" wide.

Row 1 (Right side}**:** Dc in next 8 sts, work Popcorn in next st, dc in next 8 sts.

Row 2: Hdc in next 17 sts.

Row 3: Dc in next 5 hdc, (work Popcorn in next hdc, dc in next 5 hdc) twice.

Row 4: Hdc in next 17 sts.

Row 5: Dc in next 3 hdc, work Popcorn in next hdc, dc in next 9 hdc, work Popcorn in next hdc, dc in next 3 hdc.

Row 6: Hdc in next 17 sts.

Row 7: Dc in next hdc, work Popcorn in next hdc, dc in next 13 hdc, work Popcorn in next hdc, dc in next hdc.

Row 8: Hdc in next 17 sts.

Row 9: Dc in next 2 hdc, work Popcorn in next hdc, (dc in next 5 hdc, work Popcorn in next hdc) twice, dc in next 2 hdc.

Row 10: Hdc in next 17 sts.

Row 11: Dc in next 5 hdc, (work Popcorn in next hdc, dc in next 5 hdc) twice.

Row 12: Hdc in next 17 sts.

Row 13: Dc in next 17 hdc.

Row 14: Hdc in next 17 dc.

Repeat Rows 1-14 for pattern.

AFGHAN

Ch 208 **loosely**.

Row 1 (Right side): Sc in second ch from hook and in each ch across: 207 sc.

Row 2: Ch 3, turn; dc in next sc and in each sc across.

Row 3: Ch 3, turn; work Row 1 of Ridge Panel, work Row 1 of Popcorn Panel, work Row 1 of Ridge Panel, ★ work Row 1 of Cable Panel, work Row 1 of Ridge Panel, work Row 1 of Heart Panel, work Row 1 of Ridge Panel, work Row 1 of Cable Panel, work Row 1 of Ridge Panel, work Row 1 of Popcorn Panel, work Row 1 of Ridge Panel; repeat from ★ 2 times **more**, work FPdc around turning ch.

Row 4: Ch 3, turn; work **next** row of Ridge Panel, work **next** row of Popcorn Panel, work **next** row of Ridge Panel, ★ work **next** row of Cable Panel, work **next** row of Ridge Panel, work **next** row of Heart Panel, work **next** row of Ridge Panel, work **next** row of Cable Panel, work **next** row of Ridge Panel, work **next** row of Popcorn Panel, work next row of Ridge Panel; repeat from ★ 2 times **more**, work FPdc around turning ch.

Repeat Row 4 until Afghan measures approximately 50" from beginning chain, ending by working Row 12 of Heart Panel.

Last Row: Ch 3, turn; dc in next st and in each st across; do **not** finish off.

EDGING

Rnd 1: Ch 1, turn; sc evenly around entire afghan, working 3 sc in each corner; join with slip st to first sc.

Rnd 2: Ch 1, do **not** turn; sc in same st, ch 5, (skip next sc, sc in next sc, ch 5) around; join with slip st to first sc, finish off.

Tree of Life

Finished Size: Approximately 38" x 50"

MATERIALS

Baby Sport Weight Yarn, approximately:
36 ounces, (1020 grams, 4,525 yards)
Crochet hook, size E (3.50 mm) **or** size needed for gauge

GAUGE: 15 Dc and 7 rows = 3"

PATTERN STITCHES

Note: See Stitch Directory, pages 14-16.

BASKET WEAVE PANEL (multiple of 4 + 2 sts)
Note: 10 Stitch panel should be 2" wide.
14 Stitch should be 2¾" wide.

Row 1: Work FPdc around next 2 sts, ★ work BPdc around next 2 sts. work FPdc around 2 sts; repeat from ★across.

Repeat Row 1 for pattern.

HONEYCOMB PANEL (20 sts)
Note: Panel should be 3¼" wide.

Row 1 (Right side)**:** Work BPdc around next 2 sts, work F2 Cable, work BPdc around next 2 sts, work FPdc around next 2 sts, work F4 Cable, work FPdc around next 2 sts, work BPdc around next 2 sts, work F2 Cable, work BPdc around next 2 sts.

Row 2: Work FPdc around next 2 sts, work BPdc around next 2 sts, work FPdc around next 2 sts, work BPdc around next 8 sts, work FPdc around next 2 sts, work BPdc around next 2 sts, work FPdc around next 2 sts.

Row 3: Work BPdc around next 2 sts, work F2 Cable, work BPdc around next 2 sts, work B4 Cable, work F4 Cable, work BPdc around next 2 sts, work F2 Cable, work BPdc around next 2 sts.

Row 4: Repeat Row 2.

Row 5: Work BPdc around next 2 sts, work F2 Cable, work BPdc around next 2 sts, work FPdc around next 2 sts, dc in next 4 sts, work FPdc around next 2 sts, work BPdc around next 2 sts, work F2 Cable, work BPdc around next 2 sts.

Row 6: (Work FPdc around next 2 sts, work BPdc around next 2 sts) twice, dc in next 4 dc, (work BPdc around next 2 sts, work FPdc around next 2 sts) twice.

Row 7: Work BPdc around next 2 sts, work F2 Cable, work BPdc around next 2 sts, work F4 Cable, work B4 Cable, work BPdc around next 2 sts, work F2 Cable, work BPdc around next 2 sts.

Row 8: Repeat Row 2.

Repeat Rows 1-8 for pattern.

TREE PANEL (13 sts)
Note: Panel should be $2^1/_2$" wide.

Row 1 (Right side)**:** Dc in next 4 dc, work B2 Twist, work FPdc around next dc, work F2 Twist, dc in next 4 dc.

Row 2: Dc in next 4 dc, work BPdc around next st, (dc in next dc, work BPdc around next st) twice, dc in next 4 dc.

Row 3: Dc in next 3 dc, work B2 Twist, dc in next dc, work FPdc around next st, dc in next dc, work F2 Twist, dc in next 3 dc.

Row 4: Dc in next 3 dc, work BPdc around next st, (dc in next 2 dc, work BPdc around next st) twice, dc in next 3 dc.

Row 5: Dc in next 2 dc, work B2 Twist, dc in next 2 dc, work FPdc around next st, dc in next 2 dc, work F2 Twist, dc in next 2 dc.

Row 6: Dc in next 2 dc, work BPdc around next st, (dc in next 3 dc, work BPdc around next st) twice, dc in next 2 dc.

Row 7: Dc in next dc, work B2 Twist, dc in next 3 dc, work FPdc around next st, dc in next 3 dc, work F2 Twist, dc in next dc.

Row 8: Dc in next dc, work BPdc around next st, (dc in next 4 dc, work BPdc around next st) twice, dc in next dc.

Row 9: Work B2 Twist, dc in next 2 dc, work B2 Twist, work FPdc around next st, work F2 Twist, dc in next 2 dc, work F2 Twist.

Row 10: Work BPdc around next st, dc in next 3 dc, work BPdc around next st, (dc in next dc, work BPdc around next st) twice, dc in next 3 dc, work BPdc around next st.

Repeat Rows 3-10 for pattern.

AFGHAN

Ch 210 **loosely**.

Row 1 (Right side)**:** Sc in second ch from hook and in each ch across: 209 sc.

Row 2: Ch 3, turn; dc in next sc and in each sc across.

Row 3: Ch 3, turn; work Row 1 of Basket Weave Panel across next 10 sts, work Row 1 of Honeycomb Panel, work Row 1 of Tree Panel, work Row 1 of Homeycomb Panel, ★ work Row 1 of Basket Weave Panel across next 14 sts, work Row 1 of Honeycomb Panel, work Row 1 of Tree Panel, work Row 1 of Honeycomb Panel; repeat from ★ once **more**, work Row 1 of Basket Weave Panel across next 10 sts, work FPdc around turning ch.

Row 4: Ch 3, turn; work **next** row of Basket Weave Panel across next 10 sts, work **next** row of Honeycomb Panel, work **next** row of Tree Panel, work **next** row of Honeycomb Panel, ★ work **next** row of Basket Weave Panel across next 14 sts, work **next** row of Honeycomb Panel, work **next** row of Tree Panel, work **next** row of Honeycomb Panel; repeat from ★ once **more**, work **next** row of Basket Weave Panel across next 10 sts, work FPdc around turning ch.

Repeat Row 4 until Afghan measures approximately 49" from beginning chain, ending by working Row 2 of Honeycomb Panel.

Last Row: Ch 3, turn; dc in next st and in each st across; do **not** finish off.

EDGING

Note: Decreases are made as follows: Pull up a loop in next 2 sts, YO and draw through all 3 loops on hook.

Rnd 1: Ch 1, do **not** turn; working in end of rows, work 264 sc evenly spaced across to beginning ch; working in free loops of beginning ch, 3 sc in first ch, sc in next 3 chs, (decrease, sc in next 2 chs) across to last ch, 3 sc in last ch; working in end of rows, work 264 sc evenly spaced across; working across last row, 3 sc in first dc, sc in next 3 dc, (decrease, sc in next 2 dc) across to last st, 3 sc in last st; join with slip st to first sc: 852 sc.

Rnd 2: Turn; slip st in next 2 sc, ch 1, sc in same st, ch 5, (skip next 2 sc, sc in next sc, ch 5) around to last 2 sc, skip last 2 sc; join with slip st to first sc, finish off.

Twists & Turns

Finished Size: Approximately 36" x 50"

MATERIALS

Baby Sport Weight Yarn, approximately:
29 ounces, (820 grams, 3,645 yards)
Crochet hook, size E (3.50 mm) **or** size needed for gauge

GAUGE: 15 Dc and 7 rows = 3"

PATTERN STITCHES

Note: See Stitch Directory, pages 14-16.

POPCORN PANEL (17 sts)
Note: Panel should be 3" wide.

Row 1 (Right side)**:** Work BPdc around next 2 dc, work B2 Twist, work F2 Twist, work BPdc around next 2 dc, work Popcorn in next dc, work BPdc around next 2 dc, work B2 Twist, work F2 Twist, work BPdc around next 2 dc.

Row 2: Work FPdc around next 2 sts, work BPdc around next st, dc in next 2 dc, work BPdc around next st, work FPdc around next 2 sts, ch 1, skip next Popcorn, work FPdc around next 2 sts, work BPdc around next st, dc in next 2 dc, work BPdc around next st, work FPdc around next 2 sts.

Row 3: Work BPdc around next 2 sts, work B2 Twist, work F2 Twist, work BPdc around next 2 sts, work Popcorn in next ch-1 sp, work BPdc around next 2 sts, work B2 Twist, work F2 Twist, work BPdc around next 2 sts.

Repeat Rows 2 and 3 for pattern.

BRAIDED PANEL (9 sts)
Note: Panel should be 1½" wide.

Row 1 (Right side)**:** Work B6 Cable, work FPdc around next 3 sts.

Row 2: Work BPdc around next 9 sts.

Row 3: Work FPdc around next 3 sts, work F6 Cable.

Row 4: Work PBdc around next 9 sts.

Repeat Rows 1-4 for pattern.

LATTICE PANEL (24 sts)
Note: Panel should be 4¼" wide.

Row 1 (Right side)**:** Dc in next 2 dc, work F4 Cable, (dc in next 4 dc, work F4 Cable) twice, dc in next 2 dc.

Row 2: Dc in next 2 dc, work BPdc around next 4 sts, (dc in next 4 dc, work BPdc around next 4 sts) twice, dc in next 2 dc.

Row 3: (Work B4 Twist, work F4 Twist) 3 times.

Row 4: Work BPdc around next 2 sts, dc in next 4 dc, (work BPdc around next 4 sts, dc in next 4 dc) twice, work BPdc around next 2 sts.

Row 5: Work FPdc around next 2 sts, dc in next 4 dc, (work F4 Cable, dc in next 4 dc) twice, work FPdc around next 2 sts.

Row 6: Work BPdc around next 2 sts, dc in next 4 dc, (work BPdc around next 4 sts, dc in next 4 dc) twice, work BPdc around next 2 sts.

Row 7: (Work F4 Twist, work B4 Twist) 3 times.

Row 8: Dc in next 2 dc, work BPdc around next 4 sts, (dc in next 4 dc, work BPdc around next 4 sts) twice, dc in next 2 sts.

Repeat Rows 1-8 for pattern.

AFGHAN

Ch 195 **loosely**.

Row 1 (Right side)**:** Sc in second ch from hook and in each ch across: 194 sc.

Row 2: Ch 3, turn; dc in next sc and in each sc across.

Row 3: Ch 3, turn; work Row 1 of Popcorn Panel, work Row 1 of Lattice Panel, work Row 1 of Popcorn Panel, ★ work Row 1 of Braided Panel, work Row 1 of Popcorn Panel, work Row 1 of Lattice Panel, work Row 1 of Popcorn Panel; repeat from ★ once **more**, work FPdc around turning ch.

Row 4: Ch 3, turn; work **next** row of Popcorn Panel, work **next** row of Lattice Panel, work **next** row of Popcorn Panel, ★ work **next** row of Braided Panel, work **next** row of Popcorn Panel, work **next** row of Lattice Panel, work **next** row of Popcorn Panel; repeat from ★ once **more**, work FPdc around turning ch.

Repeat Row 4 until Afghan measures approximately 47" from beginning chain, ending by working Row 1 of Lattice Panel.

Next Row: Ch 3, turn; dc in next st and in each st across; do **not** finish off.

EDGING

Note: Decreases are made as follows: Pull up a loop in next 2 sts, YO and draw through all 3 loops on hook.

Rnd 1: Ch 1, turn; 3 sc in first dc, (decrease, sc in next 2 dc) across to last st, 3 sc in last st; working in end of rows, work 201 sc evenly spaced across; working in free loops of beginning ch, 3 sc in first, ch, (decrease, sc in next 2 chs) across to last ch, 3 sc in last ch; working in end of rows, work 201 sc evenly spaced across; join with slip st to first sc: 702 sc.

Rnd 2: Do **not** turn; slip st in next sc, ch 1, sc in same st, (ch 5, skip next 2 sc, sc in next sc) 49 times, ch 5, sc in **same** st (corner loop), (ch 5, skip next 2 sc, sc in next sc) 68 times, ch 5, sc in **same** st (corner loop), (ch 5, skip next 2 sc, sc in next sc) 49 times, ch 5, sc in **same** st (corner loop), (ch 5, skip next 2 sc, sc in next sc) 67 times, ch 5, skip last 2 sc, sc in same st as first sc, ch 2, dc in first sc to form last corner loop.

Rnds 3 and 4: Ch 1, sc in same loop, ch 5, ★ (sc in next loop, ch 5) across to next corner loop, (sc, ch 5) twice in corner loop; repeat from ★ 2 times **more**, (sc in next loop, ch 5) across, sc in same loop as first sc, ch 2, dc in first sc to form last loop.

Note #1: Work Picot as follows: Ch 3, slip st in third ch from hook.

Note #2: Work V-St as follows: (Dc, work Picot, dc) in sc indicated.

Row 5: Ch 1, (sc, work Picot, sc) in last loop, ★ work V-St in next sc, (sc in next loop, work V-St in next sc) across to next corner loop, (sc, work Picot, sc) in corner loop; repeat from ★ 2 times **more**, work V-St in next sc, (sc in next loop, work V-St in next sc) across; join with slip st to first sc, finish off.

General Instructions

ABBREVIATIONS

B	Back	mm	millimeters
BPdc	Back Post double crochet(s)	Rnd(s)	Round(s)
		sc	single crochet(s)
ch(s)	chain(s)	sp(s)	space(s)
dc	double crochet(s)	st(s)	stitch(es)
F	Front	tr	treble crochet(s)
FPdc	Front Post double crochet(s)	YO	yarn over
FPtr	Front Post treble crochet(s)		
hdc	half double crochet(s)		

★ — work instructions following ★ as many **more** times as indicated in addition to the first time.
† to † — work all instructions from first † to second † **as many** times as specified.
( ) — work enclosed instructions **as many** times as specified by the number immediately following **or** work all enclosed instructions in the stitch or space indicated **or** contains explanatory remarks.

GAUGE

Correct gauge is essential for proper size. Hook size given in instructions is merely a guide and should never be used without first making a sample swatch approximately 3" square in the stitch, yarn, and hook specified. Then measure it, counting your stitches and rows carefully.
If your swatch is smaller than specified, try again with a larger size hook; if larger, try again with a smaller size. Keep trying until you find the size that will give you the specified gauge. DO NOT HESITATE TO CHANGE HOOK SIZE TO OBTAIN CORRECT GAUGE.

HINTS

As in all crocheted pieces, good finishing techniques make a big difference in the quality of the piece. Make a habit of taking care of loose ends as you work. To keep loose ends from showing, always weave them back through several stitches or work over them. When ends are secure, clip them off close to work.

Stitch Directory

POPCORN

Work 5 dc in st or sp indicated, drop loop from hook, insert hook in first dc of 5-dc group, hook dropped loop ***(Fig. 1)*** and draw through.

Fig. 1

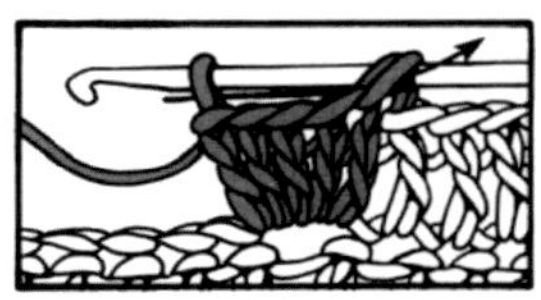

BPdc

YO, insert hook from **back** to **front** around post of st indicated ***(Fig. 2a)***, YO and pull up a loop ***(Fig. 2b)***, (YO and draw through 2 loops on hook) twice.

Fig. 2a

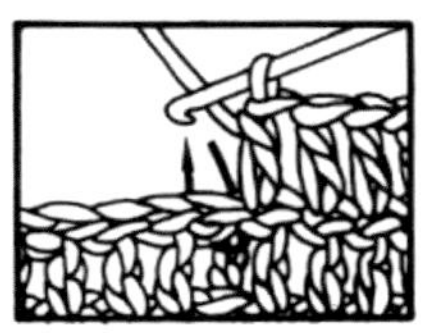

Fig. 2b

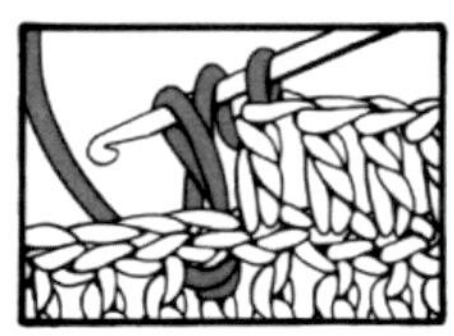

FPdc

YO, insert hook from **front** to **back** around post of st indicated ***(Fig. 3a)***, YO and pull up a loop ***(Fig. 3b)***, (YO and draw through 2 loops on hook) twice.

Fig. 3a

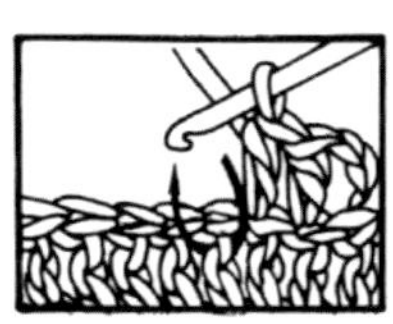

Fig. 3b

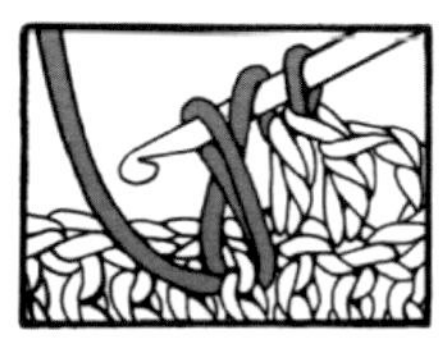

FPtr

YO twice, insert hook from **front** to **back** around post of st indicated ***(Fig. 4a)***, YO and pull up a loop ***(Fig. 4b)***, (YO and draw through 2 loops on hook) 3 times.

Fig. 4a

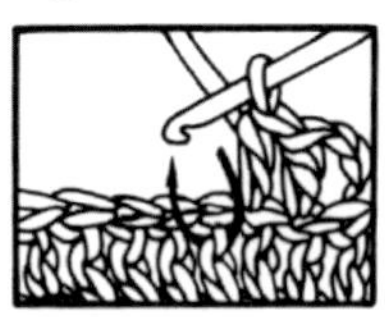

Fig. 4b

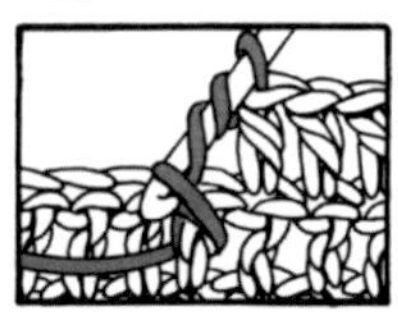

CABLE STITCHES

B4 CABLE

Skip next 2 sts, work FPtr around next 2 sts ***(Fig. 5a)***; working **behind** sts just worked, work FPtr around 2 skipped sts ***(Fig. 5b)***.

Fig. 5a

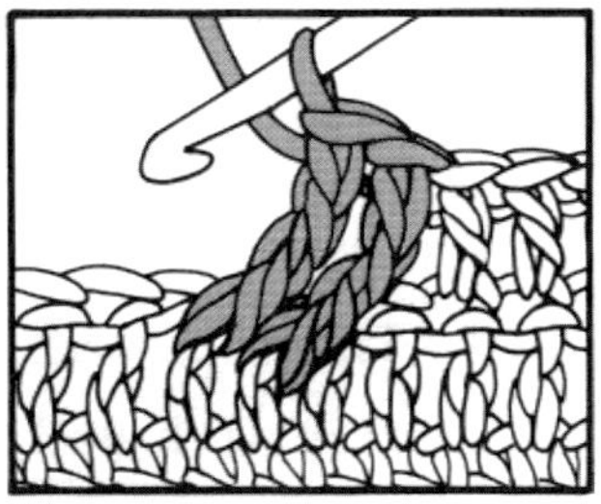

Fig. 5b

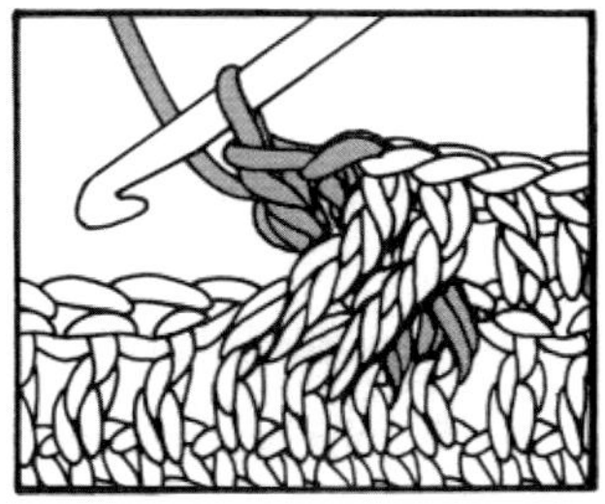

B6 CABLE

Skip next 3 sts, work FPtr around next 3 sts ***(Fig. 6a)***; working **behind** sts just worked, work FPtr around 3 skipped sts ***(Fig. 6b)***.

Fig. 6a

Fig. 6b

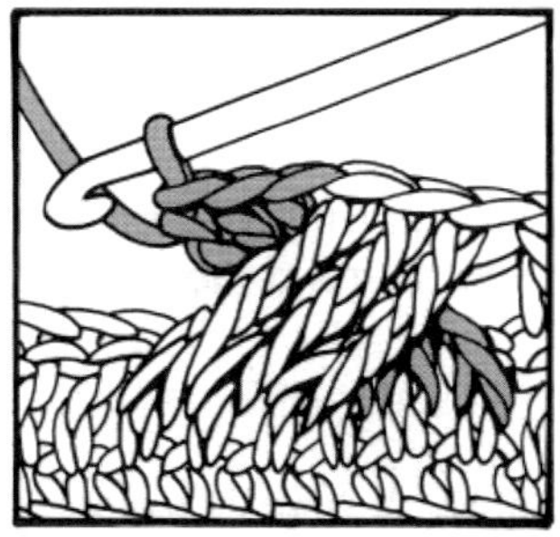

F2 CABLE

Skip next st, work FPtr around next st ***(Fig. 7a)***; working in **front** of st just worked, work FPtr around skipped st ***(Fig. 7b)***.

Fig. 7a

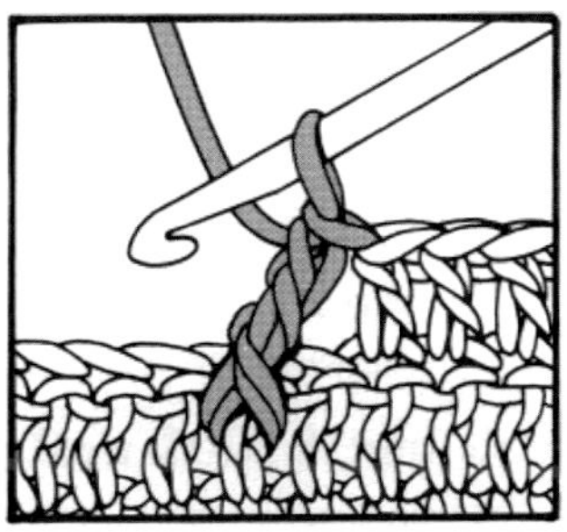

Fig. 7b

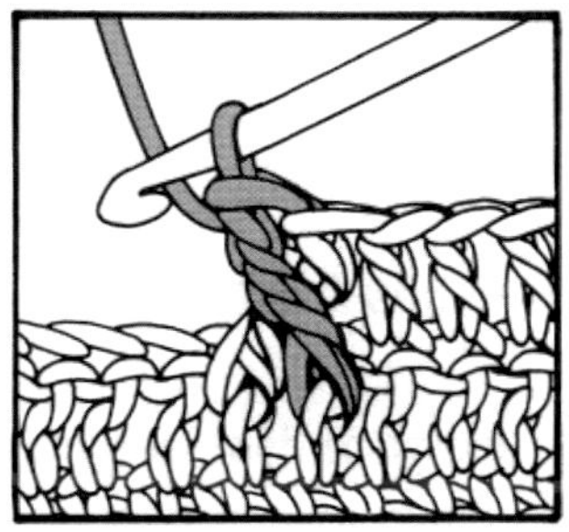

F4 CABLE

Skip next 2 sts, work FPtr around next 2 sts ***(Fig. 8a)***; working in **front** of sts just worked, work FPtr around 2 skipped sts ***(Fig. 8b)***.

Fig. 8a

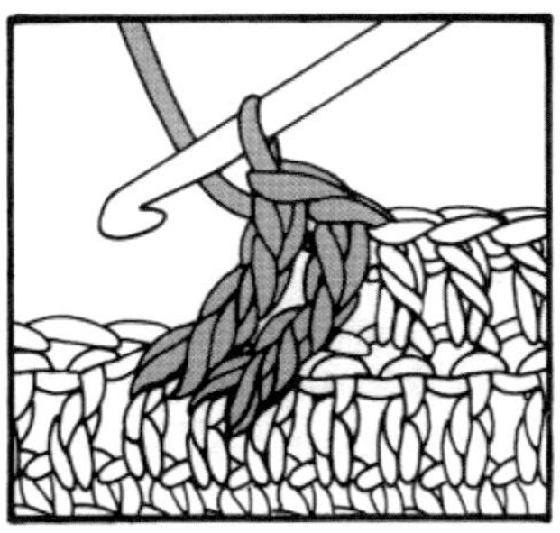

Fig. 8b

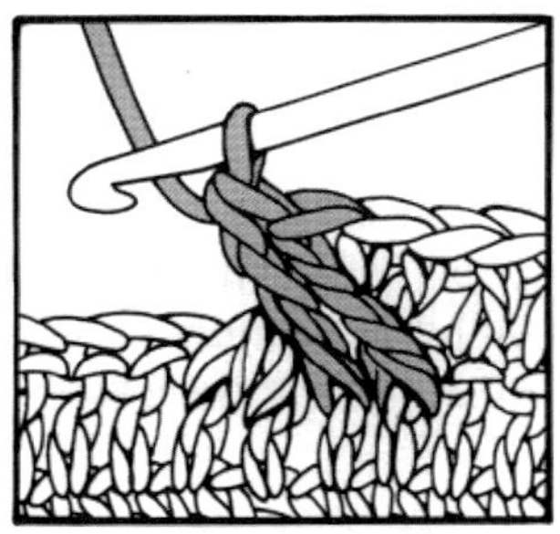

F6 CABLE

Skip next 3 sts, work FPtr around next 3 sts ***(Fig. 9a)***; working in **front** of sts just worked, work FPtr around 3 skipped sts ***(Fig. 9b)***.

Fig. 9a

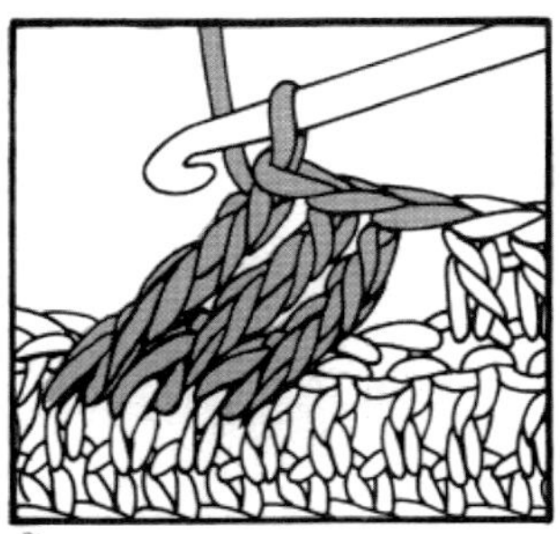

Fig. 9b

TWIST STITCHES

B2 TWIST

Skip next st, work FPtr around next st ***(Fig. 10a)***; working **behind** st just worked, dc in skipped st ***(Fig. 10b)***.

Fig. 10a

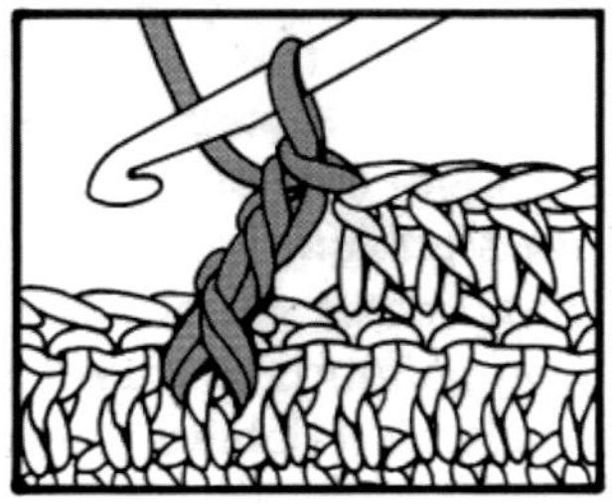

Fig. 10b

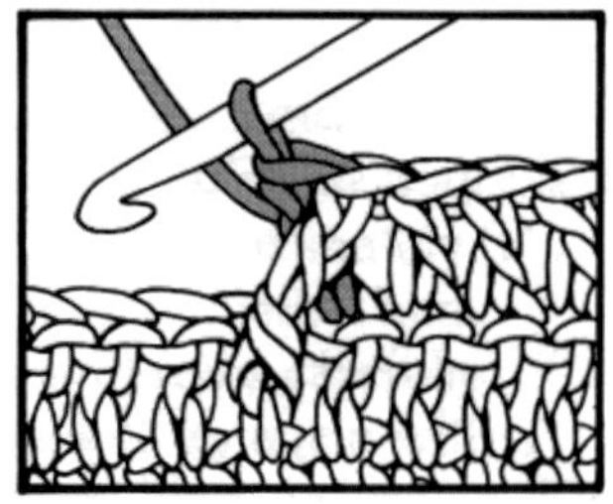

B4 TWIST

Skip next 2 sts, work FPtr around next 2 sts ***(Fig. 11a)***; working **behind** sts just worked, dc in 2 skipped sts ***(Fig. 11b)***.

Fig. 11a

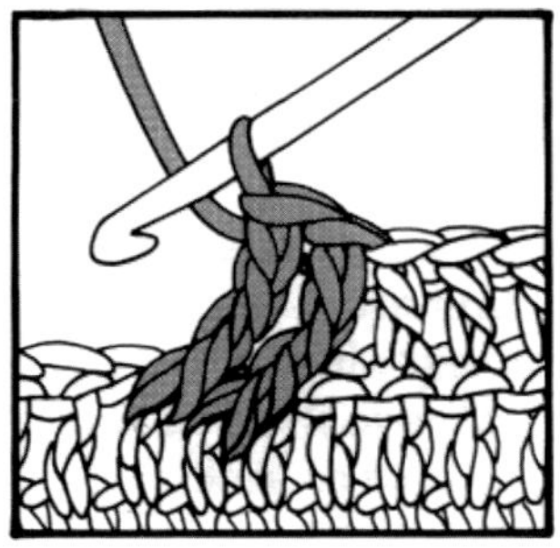

Fig. 11b

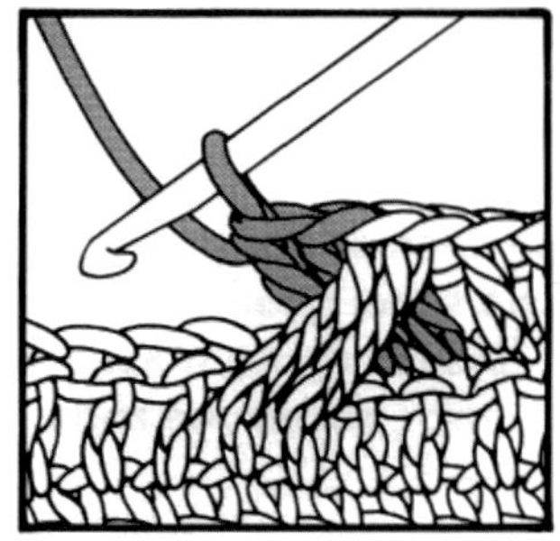

F2 TWIST

Skip next st, dc in next st ***(Fig. 12a)***; working in **front** of st just worked, work FPtr around skipped st ***(Fig. 12b)***.

Fig. 12a

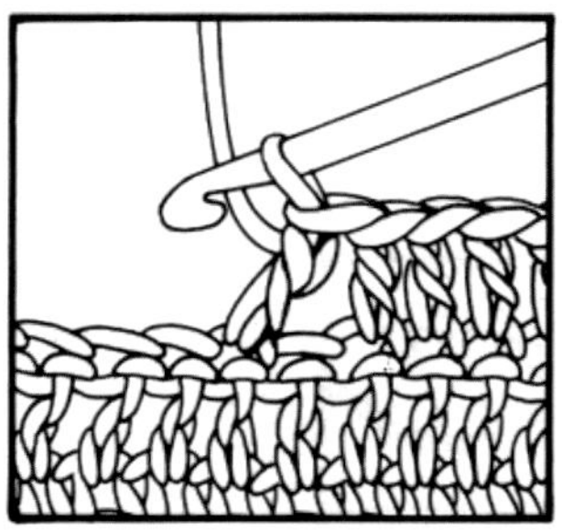

Fig. 12b

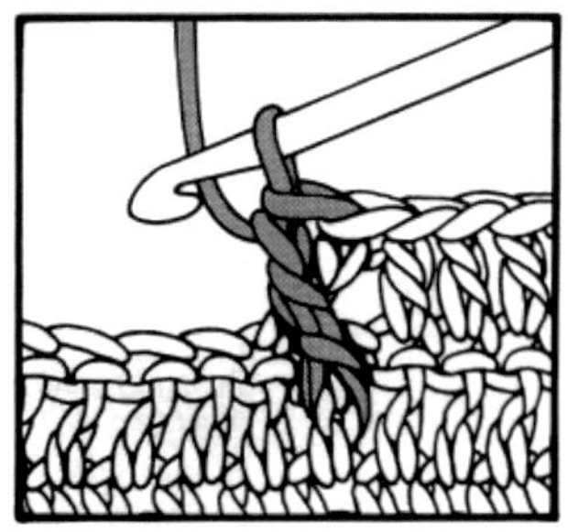

F4 TWIST

Skip next 2 sts, dc in next 2 sts ***(Fig. 13a)***; working in **front** of sts just worked, work FPtr around 2 skipped sts ***(Fig. 13b)***.

Fig. 13a

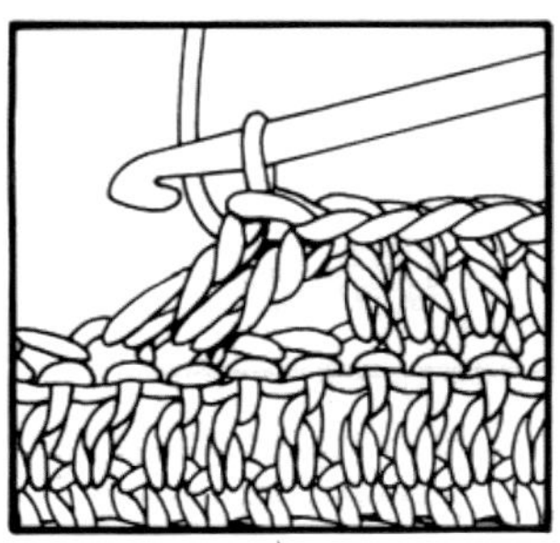

Fig. 13b

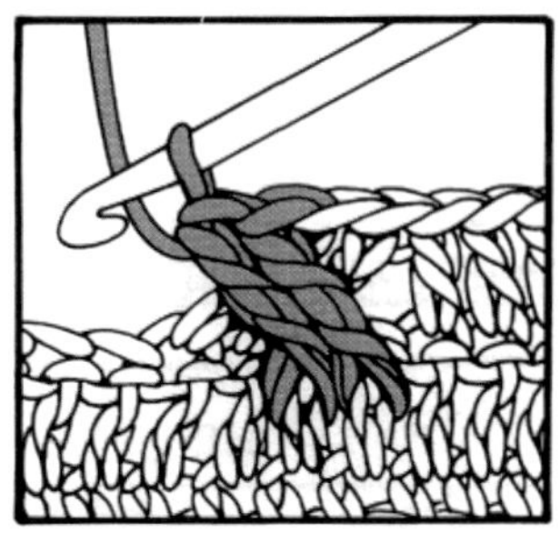